break
your
glass
slippers

amanda lovelace

break
your
glass
slippers

amanda lovelace

Andrews McMeel
PUBLISHING®

books by amanda lovelace

the

WOMEN *are some* **KIND of MAGIC**

series:

the princess saves herself in this one (#1)
the witch doesn't burn in this one (#2)
the mermaid's voice returns in this one (#3)

slay those dragons: a journal for writing your own story

***

the
things that h(a)unt
duology:

to make monsters out of girls (#1)
to drink coffee with a ghost (#2)

***

the
you are your own fairy tale
series:

break your glass slippers (#1)

for those who
break glass slippers
as well as glass ceilings.

trigger warning

this book contains
sensitive material relating to:

child abuse,
toxic friendships,
toxic romantic relationships,
sexual harassment,
eating disorders,
fatphobia,
suicide,
trauma,

& possibly more.

remember to practice self-care
before, during, & after
reading.

contents

foreword

When I was a child, I learned fairy tales are dangerous. If you believe in them too much as they are, you may find yourself under a darker spell of your own devising—wishing for princes and hoping someone saves you from the troubles in your life. It was only a few years ago, when I stumbled onto amanda lovelace's luminous work on a cold, foggy English evening in a bookstore, that I realized how empowering fairy tales can be.

In *break your glass slippers*, amanda brings to life a story that many of us have loved as children and questioned as we got older. Her words exquisitely bind the contemporary with the traditional, creating a lyrical tale of hope, inner power, and fearlessness.

The Cinderella in this book is a survivor in every way. She rises from the depths of an abyss created by despair and becomes a force to be reckoned with—all while showing us how there is strength in vulnerability and true courage in accepting who you are.

The message in this captivating book of poetry is clear: take this modern fairy tale, treasure it, and share it with someone you love. Let it teach you that the magic you are looking for already rests inside you, waiting for a spark. Let it remind you of your spirit through mystical words that awaken the flames inside you.

Here, we all get to be Cinderella, our own Fairy Godmother, and best of all, our own Prince.

May the magic help you build your own happily ever after.

May your soul feel full and bright when it does.

Nikita xxx

a note from the author

at the heart of this poetry collection is a retelling of one of the world's most recognizable & beloved fairy tales, *cinderella*. in that way, i suppose you might consider this to be a work of fiction. however, this story is also very much based on a number of my own lived experiences, as well as experiences i know to be true for many.

she is cinderella.

i am cinderella.

you may even be cinderella, too, if you find that any part of this story happens to speak to you.

laced with love,
amanda

let me tell you a sad story

there is a girl who
sings only when
every window
is shut.

like most girls,
she's been learning
the trait of silence
since birth.

everyone
underestimates
how important
her voice is,

& the greatest
tragedy of all is
that she does,
too.

let me tell you an even sadder story

there is a girl who
dances only when
every curtain
is closed.

like most girls,
she's been learning
the trait of invisibility
since birth.

no one
ever bothers
to see how
special she is,

so she
decides to dance
with her own
shadow.

i

once there lived a man who gifted his daughter
a pair of glass slippers. she clutched them to
her chest, tears welling up in her eyes. it was
then that he spoke, "these were made with my
two hands, some sweat, & a sprinkle of fairy
dust. they'll always fit you, even if you grow
taller than a beanstalk. they'll never slip, even
if you're forced to walk over ice all night long.
best of all, they'll never, ever break, except in
the case of an emergency.

whenever she walks past, the boys whisper to each other, "be on the lookout for ugly ducklings like her. treat her badly now & you risk her forgetting all about you once she transforms into a beautiful swan." none of them ever considered the fact that she could hear what they were saying.

—*she heard everything.*

fairy godmother says

it has
never been
within
your duty
to be
pretty.

"no one could ever want a fat girl like you."

—*stepmother.*

fairy godmother says

you don't need to look a certain way
to deserve someone's heart.

no matter your shape—
no matter your size—

be proud of all the space
your body dares to take up.

there are sisters
who see each other
as lifelong
rivals

when they should be
seeing each other
as lifelong
allies,

which is to say:
some sisters
are no sisters
at all.

—*she had to learn this the hard way.*

fairy godmother says

some people are simply committed to being unkind, & it is *not* your job to convince them to change. all you can do is give them all the kindness you have, & if they don't return it, then they aren't worth your sugar.

isn't the love
of a family
supposed
to be

unconditional?
unbreakable?

*if they don't
love me,
then who
ever could?*

she thinks
to herself.

—the first heartbreak.

fairy godmother says

i don't know if anyone
has ever told you this, but:

their lack of love for you
does not make you
any less loveable.

inside the cramped fitting room, she slips into
dress after dress as if she's trying to slip into
someone else's life.

—*much to her dismay, her reflection stays the same.*

fairy godmother says

when you spend
all your time
imagining yourself
in other people's shoes,

your own story
goes unwritten,

& there is nothing
more painful
than that.

every night when she's finally alone, she takes a red marker & circles the parts of herself she would most like to see disappear—*her thighs, her stomach, her upper arms*—until there's no part of her left untouched.

—*"nothing will ever be enough," she whispers.*

fairy godmother says

some days,
your body will feel like a cage.

on those days,
lace flowers through the bars.

whenever somebody asks her how she's been holding up, she can never bring herself to tell them how she's truly feeling inside. it's always *fine* or *great* or *amazing, but how are* you? the last thing she would ever want to do is inconvenience them—or worse, seem self-involved.

—*she just wants one person to catch her in the lie.*

fairy godmother says

speak your truth—
no matter what.

afterward,
take careful note

of who not only
listens

but steps up to
applaud your bravery.

there are times when she sees another girl on
the train or in a magazine & she can't be sure
what she wants to do:

    i. become her.
    ii. be her best friend.
    iii. kiss her.

—*kaleidoscope.*

fairy godmother says

who you want to kiss
is not a problem

as long as you
get permission first.

"if you want to wear the crop top, then wear the crop top. if anyone dares to point out your stretch marks or the size of your belly, just remind them that our bodies were all crafted from the same handful of stardust, & isn't that just wonderful? isn't that so special?"

—*her best friend.*

fairy godmother says

there is something
almost unearthly
about the friendship
between two girls,
isn't there?

all they ever want to do is
protect, protect, protect.
fiercely now.
fiercely now.

my advice for you:
don't take her for granted.

ever.

he has the best laugh,
forever-untied shoes,
& a heart bigger
than a blue whale's.

she only wishes
she could love him
the way he loves her,
but she can't.

when she tells him,
he explains to her
that she *owes* it to him
to love him back.

—*the boy with all the wrong intentions.*

fairy godmother says

villains almost never look like cackling witches, cruel stepmothers, or bratty stepsisters. they're so much quieter than that, & i think that's what makes them so menacing. in some chapters of your storybook, you'll find them hiding everywhere—even in the faces of those you hold dearest. they never reveal their true intentions until you've already trusted them too much, & just like that, everyone you know has turned into a stranger.

she's always checking in on people, even though they never do the same in return. whether they simply don't care enough or consider her to be better armored for this life than they are, she's not entirely certain. sometimes her mind goes to the darkest of places—that place where she wonders if any of them would notice if she disappeared altogether one night.

—*forgotten.*

fairy godmother says

without you here,

the moon & the stars
would fall.

mountains would crack
down the middle.

castles would crumble
into nothingness.

books would burst
into flames.

it's not time to go just yet.

where does she go
whenever she's feeling
deeply, deeply
blue?

up into the clouds,
filling her head with
fanciful ideas of what
her future looks like:

the clearest sky.
a handsome man in a suit.
a house with halls wide enough
for their children to run down.

—*her biggest mistake is forgetting herself along the way.*

fairy godmother says

you are limitless.

you can have the lipstick.
you can have the sword.

there's a story she's been telling herself ever since she was a little girl. in order to create her, a witch had to pour a bunch of ingredients into her bubbling cauldron—things like glitter, courage, & a hunger for fairy tales with happy endings. nowadays, she finds herself wondering if the witch forgot the most important ingredient of them all: the thing that would have made her *good enough*.

—*potion*.

fairy godmother says

it's not an easy thing
to accept yourself the way you are.

some people spend their entire lives
trying to master it.

but if anyone is strong enough
to face the challenge,

it's *you*.

it was as if she was born into this world invisible & he was the first one to notice her—to truly *see* her. after a lifetime of dancing with her own shadow, she'd found someone who could keep in perfect time with her.

finally, *finally*.

—*the ~~unseen~~ girl*.

fairy godmother says

more forgetting time.
more midnight dances with yourself.

more, always more.

she wants nothing more
than to be the kind of girl
worthy of standing
next to him.

—*she doesn't always want what's best for her.*

fairy godmother says

he is not the standard by which you should be measuring your worth in this world. before he came along, you were a fierce wonder to behold. you will continue to be that long after he walks away from you.

her heart
is a gilded thing.

his hands
were made to melt.

together,
they drip liquid gold.

—*she doesn't care if it burns.*

fairy godmother says

he may have a pretty face,
but that doesn't mean he isn't dangerous.

as though she's been put under an enchantment, she constantly finds herself smiling at odd times of the day. for the first time, it's not due to daydreams of a brave prince on a white horse or a fearsome princess with a sword.

with him, it's the real thing.

—*at least, that's what she keeps telling herself.*

fairy godmother says

infatuation is not love,

just like a love potion
is only temporary

& often causes
more harm than good.

a unicorn,
he calls her—

a miracle,
he calls her—

for somehow
managing

to remain
untouched

by another
boy.

—she wonders why she can't be magical either way.

fairy godmother says

you are not a thing
that can ever be
claimed, conquered,
or irreparably ruined
by someone else's hands.

he may like to think
he wields that much power,

but he doesn't.

"you're too good for me."

—*charming.*

fairy godmother says

people have a habit of
telling on themselves;
most of the time,
by accident.

you'll see it in
one wrong word,
or how they react when
they think no one's looking.

don't ever take it
lightheartedly,
for there is always some
truth in these moments.

be sure to armor your
kind, kind heart.
be trusting,
but be vigilant.

there's this literary cliché where a character will, in the middle of a tense conversation, suddenly let out a breath they didn't realize they'd been holding. *how can they just forget to breathe? breathing is automatic,* she always thought to herself. then she meets him & quickly finds out that it's not that ridiculous of a notion. the truth is, even the way he holds the steering wheel makes her forget she has lungs.

—sometimes the impossible is possible.

fairy godmother says

while you're getting drunk on him,

he's only getting drunk
on the way the attention
makes him feel—

there's a difference.

she's so giddy
at the very thought of him
she tosses & turns
for hours.

meanwhile,
he's sleeping soundly.

—*moonlight through glass.*

fairy godmother says

you deserve so much more
than you've been given,
so don't you dare forget
to tend to yourself.

take time to sweep your corners,
dust off your bookshelves,
shake out your rugs,
& make your windows shine.

create a safe space
for yourself to go when
it feels like the whole world
has turned against you.

it's the only thing you'll ever truly
be able to count on.

she can't help but to notice that
he only pays attention to her
when he thinks she's
paying attention to
someone else.

—*especially if that person is herself.*

fairy godmother says

you keep mistaking
possessiveness for love.

it couldn't be further from that.

know this:
nobody can ever own your magic.

it is yours & yours alone.

"he's bad for you."
—*her best friend, looking out for her.*

"he's the best thing to ever happen to me."
—*her, protecting him again.*

fairy godmother says

if they make it easy
to lie about them to
everyone around you,

then that means
something is
very, very wrong.

don't ignore red flags—
they're the universe's way
of protecting you.

leaving him
then never finding love again.

—what she's been told to fear.

fairy godmother says

despite what you have heard, being alone is not this great tragedy everyone makes it out to be. if nothing else, see it as an opportunity to reintroduce yourself to yourself. to relearn who you are today. to dream up all the people you would like to be for every tomorrow to come. above all, find the value that lies in becoming your own best friend.

he tells her that she doesn't need to wear makeup. in a manner of speaking, she agrees with him: she doesn't *need* to wear it, but she does *want* to wear it.

—that should make all the difference.

fairy godmother says

keep standing up for yourself.

don't let them get used to
the idea that their opinions
should rule you.

you, my dear, rule yourself.

you wear the crown.
you sit on the throne.
you—not them.

make sure they never forget that.

she asked him
what they were.

he let out
a laugh

& said they were
nothing

until there was
less of her,

for it would be
embarrassing

to be
seen with her.

—*too much.*

fairy godmother says

repeat after me:

there can never be
too much sky.

there can never be
too many dreams.

there can never be
too much coffee.

there can never be
too many stars.

there can never be
too much *me.*

in one breath,
he calls her *perfect.*

in the next,
he points out her imperfections.

—mixed signals.

fairy godmother says

if he doesn't think you're absolutely stunning at your dirty sweats & grass-stained feet, then he sure as hell doesn't deserve you at your fancy dress & uncomfortable heels.

when he calls her by the wrong name,
she pretends she doesn't notice.

when it comes to him,
she's gotten so good at pretending

that she sometimes worries
she might be losing herself.

—*where did she go?*

fairy godmother says

if you can no longer recognize the face
reflected in the bathroom mirror, remember
this: you are ever-changing. ever-spinning, too,
just like mother earth. when you fall from the
pure exhaustion of it all, you have every means
to get back up & start over again.

keep going, little dancer.

keep going.

he always keeps her waiting, & she pretends she
doesn't mind at all, but deep down, she does.

—*read at 3:37 a.m.*

fairy godmother says

it's not a character flaw
to care too much,
but it can drain you
until you have nothing
left to give yourself.

when he comes back, he comes back missing
her body, but not her—never *her*.

—*self-portrait.*

fairy godmother says

run far, far away from anyone
who makes you feel like

you have to give them parts of yourself
you're not ready or willing to give.

doing this doesn't mean
you're a *tease*, a *prude*, or *ashamed*.

your body belongs to you
& you decide what you do with it.

after he's done telling her exactly what he knows she wants to hear, he walks away & whispers the same words into the ear of some other unsuspecting girl.

—*charming.*

fairy godmother says

use gentle words
until gentle words
no longer work.

there is such bravery in her silence.

—*ghosting.*

fairy godmother says

there is nothing in this world like the relief of
knowing that you owe answers to nobody &
nobody owes answers to you in return. we need
not tie each other into knots to please one
another. we are free to choose who we
welcome into our homes & who gets the
privilege to stay.

her precious fairy tales showed her what would happen if she found her prince, but they never prepared her for what she should do if her prince turned out to be her unhappily ever after.

—*cinderella.*

fairy godmother says

you will feel like you've made
a mess of things,

even when it's not your fault.

you will feel hopeless.
you will feel helpless.

you will consider giving up.

it is then you must remember
that you alone have the power
to clean it back up again.

after hours of sobbing into her mascara-
streaked pillow, she looks to the night sky &
asks, "where, oh where, is the fairy godmother
who will come fix my life?"

—*stargazer.*

fairy godmother says

get that head out of the stars.

here's a secret:
your fairy godmother is inside you.

you only need to
believe in her
for your every wish
to come true.

(no wand necessary.)

ii

before you turn another page, try your hardest to forget everything you know about the fairy tales you read as a child. in this fairy tale, the princess doesn't recklessly leave behind a glass slipper for the not-so-charming prince. in this fairy tale, the princess takes a hammer to them, shattering both to pieces.

i've learned that you need to learn how to dance alone for a while before you're able to find a good partner again. one who won't make you spin around in circles to get you to stay. one who will gladly let you fumble, maybe even step on their toes a little bit. one who won't try to hold you back when you run away, if that's what you feel is best for you.

—*my solo.*

it's okay if you don't think
i'm fit to be the queen to your king.

—*there are so many more important things to be.*

you were never able to
make time for me.

now that you're gone,
i make time for myself.

never have i been
more content in a relationship.

—*muted & blocked.*

when i fall asleep each night, i dream my own dreams. by some miracle, you don't make an appearance in any of them, making them all the more beautiful.

—*i only wish i'd gotten here sooner.*

you're no longer
my first thought
when i wake up
in the morning,

but i'll make sure
i'm your first thought
right before you
drift off to sleep.

you were my *almost*,
but i'm my own *forever*.

—*long may i reign.*

how does it feel to know that
i'll always be *the girl who got away*?

how does it feel to know that
you'll always be *the fuckboy who lost her*?

—*the curse.*

we all need to check in
on ourselves more.

☑ _____ have you taken a break? _____
☑ _____ have you stretched? _____
☑ _____ have you moved around? _____
☑ _____ have you eaten? _____
☑ _____ have you hydrated? _____

☑ _____ have you ignored his texts? _____
☑ _____ have you recognized your worth? _____
☑ _____ have you righted your crown? _____

time + distance + prioritizing yourself^2

—this is how you move on.

you needn't try to race the clock to find your
soul mate. trust me: they aren't going anywhere.
when—or *if*—you're ready to meet them,
they'll be waiting patiently.

so often we are our own one true love.

there is *nothing*
unfeminist
about the girl
who chooses
the ball gown
& the prince.

there is *everything*
unfeminist
about those
who try to
shame her for
her choices.

she may *have it all*,
but that doesn't
stop you from
having it all.

celebrate her,
then celebrate you.

first you must realize
you can both
be successful
in different ways.

—*internalized misogyny.*

at the same time,
you need to

be willing to
recognize your privilege.

be willing to
lace your fingers together.

be willing to
give a boost when you can.

—*we don't win till we're all winning.*

if i've learned
anything at all about
being a woman
it's that

people will champion you
until the moment
you stand up
for yourself

a little too loudly,
a little too brashly.

—*don't let that stop you from fighting for what matters.*

being called *fat* is not an insult.
being called *skinny* is not a compliment.

—they're just sizes.

i'm trying to listen to my body more. i eat whatever it needs at that moment. sometimes that means fruit, sometimes that means chocolate. there are no longer safe foods or dangerous foods. there is just *food*—the energy required for my survival, the most important thing of all. not other people's unrealistic expectations, or my own.

my value doesn't go down when my weight
goes up.

there is no
letting yourself go,

just becoming
comfortable
in your own skin.

—*it should be celebrated, not scorned.*

superficial is the person who can't imagine worshiping you at every stage of *you*.

i am not my insecure nights.
i am not my broken promises.
i am not my messiest moments.
i am not my bad decisions.

i am not that little voice inside that whispers,
"they hate you, they hate you, they hate you."

—*i am so much more.*

i. getting out of bed.
ii. remembering to eat.
iii. drinking a glass of water.
iv. being kind to yourself.
v. surviving the day.

—*reasons to be proud of yourself, big or small.*

at first, self-love can feel like you're trying to catch lightning in a bottle—next to impossible. i didn't believe i could ever hold that much power in my hands, until the day i did. ever since, i've become a terrifying storm of a girl who will never settle for anything less than what she deserves.

i'm done being afraid of
what other people think of me.

if you want to judge me,
i won't stop you.

i'll be over here,
being flawless in every flaw.

—*confidence.*

when they tell me that i've changed, like it's some personal act of betrayal on my part, i tell them, "i know. i've never been more proud of myself. i went from a single wildflower to a whole fucking meadow."

everyone in your life
should be a source of joy:
family, friends, partners—
every single person.

if you always have to
worry about them,
then it's past time to
create some boundaries.

sometimes that will mean
getting out the scissors &
cutting the very strings
that connect you.

withholding forgiveness
can be a form of self-care.

i've been facing up to difficult truths. for one, the fact that i tend to sweep aside the love i'm freely & unconditionally given from some so i can focus on the love that's missing from others instead. it's not fair to try to convince someone to care about me, or to overlook the ones who already do.

—it's time for me to break the cycle.

if you feel like you need to lower your vibration to meet someone else's, then maybe it's time to say "goodbye."

—*always protect your peace.*

i don't know who
needs to hear this, but:

it's okay if someone doesn't like you.

it doesn't mean there's
something wrong with you.

it doesn't mean there's
something wrong with them.

some kinds of magic
just don't call to each other.

strong is she
who knows when
she needs to lay
her battles down to rest.

strong is she
who knows the difference
between quitting
& self-preservation.

every full moon is a reminder
of what has come full circle
& must be released.

every new moon is a chance
to start anew.

—*cherish your every phase.*

never again will i choose
a toxic partner over a well-meaning friend.

you're allowed to hold your family at arm's length. family can be toxic. family can be abusive. family can belittle you, invalidate you, or make you feel unsafe. you don't need to explain yourself to anyone who disagrees.

—*do what you have to do.*

if you do it to protect
your mental health,
then it is not cruel,
nor is it selfish.

i've found that most *from rags to riches* stories
have very little to do with things such as money
or material objects & everything to do with
who's still standing by your side when you
discover your own self-worth.

—you're a fucking treasure.

if life is just a storybook
then i'm opening it up
to every page you're on
& ripping them out,
right down to the spine.

—*it'll be like you never existed.*

i stopped wondering
when the next chapter
would finally begin,
& i started writing it instead.

—*how i got out of my own way.*

i hereby grant myself
the permission
to not be strong
all of the time.

i also grant myself
the permission
to not be soft
all of the time.

i'm allowed to
just simply *be*.

—*temperance.*

maybe i was never given a fairy godmother who turned a pumpkin into an enchanted carriage that took me straight to my happily ever after. but i no longer make excuses, i drink pumpkin spice lattes, & i check things off my to-do list. i handle things that i never, ever could have handled before.

—if that's not a true transformation, what is?

sometimes the only difference between not being meant for something & being meant for something is the necessary journey it takes for you to get there.

—replace your self-doubt with patience.

you are never directionless.

—*the universe is always guiding you.*

wishing upon
every shooting star isn't
the way your dreams
will come true.

taking your fate
into your own hands
is how your dreams
will come true.

so
work hard.
work harder.
work even harder.

—*make it happen.*

don't worry about
all the people out there
catching fireflies
when you're out here
catching entire galaxies.

—*stay focused on your goals.*

you are the only set of keys
to your castle.

the rest of them are nothing but
bad copies.

dear prince,

if you tried to find me now, you wouldn't be able to. you see, when i finally learned how to love myself, everything about me changed.

love,
the princess

iii

she never needed anyone else's help to have the fairy tale she always wanted. at long last, she's realized one of the greatest truths a person can learn during the course of a life: *she is her own goddamn fairy tale.*

special acknowledgments

I. *my spouse, cyrus parker*—thank you for your endless support & coffee runs. <3

II. *my writing critique partners, trista mateer & christine day*—thank you for always helping me make my books what they are. i'd be lost without you two.

III. *mira kennedy*—thank you for every grammar correction.

IV. *my family*—thank you for the endless words of encouragement you give.

V. *my readers*—thank you for always reminding me that i'm never alone.

about the author

amanda lovelace is the author of the celebrated "women are some kind of magic" series. somehow, she is also the two-time winner of the goodreads choice award for best poetry, as well as a USA TODAY & *publishers weekly* bestseller. when she isn't reading, writing, or drinking a much-needed cup of coffee, you can find her casting spells from her home in a (very) small town on the jersey shore.

follow the author

🐦 @ladybookmad

📷 @ladybookmad

t @amandalovelace

🌐 amandalovelace.com

Andrews McMeel Publishing
a division of Andrews McMeel Universal
1130 Walnut Street, Kansas City, Missouri 64106

www.andrewsmcmeel.com

20 21 22 23 24 RR2 10 9 8 7 6 5 4 3 2

ISBN: 978-1-5248-5189-7

Library of Congress Control Number: 2019953169

Illustrations by Janaina Medeiros

Editor: Patty Rice
Art Director/Designer: Julie Barnes
Production Editor: David Shaw
Production Manager: Cliff Koehler